It seems as though we truly have been through

everything together

Love always,

Jack

High off the feeling of publishing my first book, *For You,* I waited little time before beginning my second project with one goal in mind: be better than the last. Writing each poem has been a quest to search for perfection, an attempt to unravel poetry before packing it all back together. There have been more late nights and crazy ideas, but what has really stood out to me throughout the production of *everything* has been the difference in my mindset.

I began *For You* at a very insecure time in my life. An early high school freshman, my emotions were irregular and I was learning so much so fast. I think I published my first poetry collection to relieve so much of what I felt – resentment, sadness, grief, and anger. That being said, *everything* has been a very different experience. One year later and the sequel is complete with a completely different style. Though the teenage heartbreak genre has continued across both stories, what lies ahead is something completely different than the last. I have everyone except myself to thank for this, especially my friends. I also think all of my friends' moms deserve some recognition for being 99% of my fan base.

The title, *everything*, had no clear meaning until I began to write. I realized that one the goals I focused on the most when writing this story was to diversify my poetry and create something even more people besides sad, moody adolescents could relate to. I've tried my best to include something for everyone.

Allow me to shout-out my amazingly talented best friend and illustrator for my book, Annabeth Bradley. Words cannot express how much I love and appreciate you and your work. You are someone I will never forget as we move through the rest of our lives and I am so glad our friendship is immortalized in these pages.

If my first book helped you, the readers, express what you felt, I'm thrilled. I hope you can relate to *everything* just as much, but hopefully in a happier, healthier way (just as I have felt happier and healthier in its creation.) This book tells many stories, but I am in firm belief that within these pages you can find something, maybe even *everything*.

everything: poetry for anyone

confessions of an artist and a poet

I tried to rhyme this. I really
did. Despite the amount of
backspaces and rhyme zone searches,
nothing ever felt right.

It's almost like drawing
I can't seem to make anything straight.
My proportions are always off
but I've chalked it up to my hand trembling.

I'm wrong, though. Truth is,
like rhyming, sometimes drawing
requires too much structure. I fail to see where
art ends and math begins and
I wonder what's wrong with me.

How much of a failure am I?
To be one who conjures words as if

the world owes him and yet
I cannot give back a song.

If you heard me reading this maybe
you would be more pleased. Sadly, my
voice only comes through on paper and
in ink.

No matter how many bumble bees
appear at the tip of my pencil, I still cannot see
something concrete. Like poetry,
drawing is allowed to be wild
until it's not.

I break format so much that I forget it even
existed at all

I listen to the buzz-headed man proclaim his
love in 1400 words and I question if I will ever
be good enough to visit Iceland or

the graveyard of artists and poets who
accomplished what I haven't yet. And will I
ever? My hand and my words and my ink grips
everything so hard. Especially my heart.

Everyone I aspire to be
could lock me in metaphors and
erase the key with the backend of a pencil.
I'd probably let them.

I'm so accustomed to
words being weapons. So I always
write against you, never *For You,*
no matter how I may deny it.

Everyone has their own ideas
about brush strokes and word choice
and what's acceptable content. On and off the
page, my work is a list
of
everything

everyone

says

I

should

do.

But perhaps I do not need rhymes or straight
lines or skylines or goodbyes. I can create what
and how I want
and no format or medium or critic can take away
what I have proven
myself to be over and over again.

Do you think I am fazed by your words that I
can and have used in love poetry?
Does your canvas carry a bolder piece of art
because it is bigger, or does it

make up for your lack of confidence. I'd smile at you but you'd mistake it for weakness so I'll just stare. And feel bad.

look at me

like a mirror, you see yourself
because i am terrified of being anything other
than the familiar:
that which you know and understand
i dream that if our eyes are identical, there's no
room
for mistakes. no time for the visions to move out
of sync
always accurately acquitted

look at me

your smile seems so
infectious, doesn't it. perhaps i know that if you
caught me toothless, we would part
when you blink, however,
then you could see me
silently, slowly smiling
as i am, not a pane of glass

but a human
glass that shatters and stings your hands
a boy who writes and performs and cries and
exists
without following your lead

for now, though
our hands can never meet,
separated by a mirror that never cracks:
it has grown so strong
reflecting that which it is not

bathe

today i turned the shower on as hot as it would
go
maybe just to feel something again
i waited until my body didn't burn
like a match right before it is extinguished

i've scrubbed my skin
hard
i'm raw and natural
i'm beginning to ache but at least i can breathe

soap fills my mouth but i still don't taste
the way a child does when they've cursed
i promised myself youth and innocence but
never received it
i hear water running from what it cannot see
i see myself in tiles, seemingly immortalized in
marble

i wrote this in my head

while my thoughts drowned

it took me so long to realize the showerhead and

i

cried in unison

his words were so light

he measured them carefully

always afraid they might float away

- **weightless**

dusk

perhaps i am trapped in the webs created by the
power lines that criss-cross over the sunset
do you see me suspended, basking in warmth i
knew was coming but still felt blissful to receive?
i've waited for you
not because i wanted to
just because i knew you'd come
like sunset, you're expected but still stunningly
beautiful
how did we meet here again?
did you time this perfectly, so that you would
catch me when i am most vulnerable
my eyes drawn to the sky instead of your hips
and smile
unable to defend myself from whatever happens
next
the buildings shine you know
maybe even more than you
why are you still talking

just look up

look away for one second

i already gave you everything else, it wasn't
enough

you didn't want my heart or my body

you wanted my words

you didn't want this sunset

you wanted to hear what i would say about it

this is all i have left for you

bright lights turning dim and sparkles where
sparkles do not live

cars moving like blurs and houses sitting boldly

power lines and the sunset

why do you watch what you don't want

please

it's too much now

why me

does it bring you joy? knowing how you control
me

do you laugh while i brush the tears out of my
eyes

or simply smile knowing even the sun isn't

enough to keep me from you

to know how the sky could open and dump a

thousand gallons on me

but i would remain here

waiting for you to return

like a sunrise

nostalgia

if i find myself in the middle of the place i've
cursed forever
the city whose days have been counted down
since i was 10
do i have anything to thank?
the car horns or the tall buildings?
the hot weather i've always been uncomfortable
in?
the people i've loved and the buildings i've been
in?
i cannot leave it all behind with only a label
i cannot pretend that i've grown up in hell
because truthfully, so much of me is here, where
i've convinced myself it doesn't want to be
given the opportunity to come back later, i swear
i wouldn't
but i would if only to ride down the streets that
felt my feet grow to size 13
to feel the wind that flew my first kite

i have run to a future that contains none of my
past
but how can i not look back for even a second
and remember the eyes i have looked into and
sworn my life would be worse without
how can i not thank this city for the people it has
given me,
for the opportunity i have received to escape if
given the choice.
to the school that i won't admit i sometimes
enjoy,
thank you. don't forget me
to the streets i wish my parents would let me
stay out later on,
i have enjoyed your asphalt more than my own
bed sheets
to the people who it seems as if i've already
forgotten
hold me once more
to this place i will eventually leave,
you will always have a piece of me

for better or for worse

built

he whispered, "i've always liked buildings"
as a boy he would watch each piece add up bit
by bit to create something greater
something unimaginably spectacular
i can see him now
a child, soon to be a man
enjoying the way things seem to change in no
time
watching the sun disappear behind a sculpture
crafted by sweat and blood
he dreams of dancing among the clouds and
looking down to admire the work he has
completed

"look at me now"
now he drives cars
vehicles that do not grow or change
crafted in factories by metal and the inhuman
seemingly trapped

he remembers

a child waiting on the road for a driver kind

enough to take him to a place he doesn't know

the name of

have you ever seen the man in the car

the one with dark hair and dark eyes

and dark dreams

clouded with dead desires and hopeless hearts

a boy drives cars now

he's barely 18 and he promises you a safe travel

if you can describes the structures you pass

"no time to look up anymore"

horizontal, never vertical

never up, always forwards

i wonder how it feels to never be in pieces

to remain a whole something that you

never wanted to be

never got his dream

never built his building

does he fear the dust that comes with
destruction?
does he know how sulfur tastes?
how bland is a life behind a wheel when one is
meant to exist behind windows

i wonder what stops him from escaping?
build on dear friend

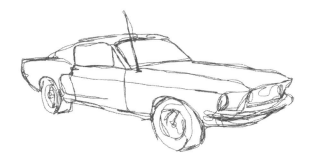

father's legacy

and since the beginning
it was always you
strong hands and a soft smile
crinkled forehead from years of laughing.
my very own superhero who took me to new
lands
and held my hand while promising me
how much he loved me
but i already knew
i was too little then to express the same emotions
and despite every tussle and argument a father
and a son can have
you remain a force to be reckoned with on every
playing field
to know your existence continues
for years
only brings me great joy
to know
that with each passing year

i am only closer
to becoming more like you.
i am so thankful
that you live within me
and i within you

i've pondered you everyday
until i realized
my mind wants to think about you
about as much as you want me
that is, not at all

- nothing and everything

There once was a boy who lived near the stars. Every night he would travel out to dance among them, to feel their rays upon his skin as he threw himself through the sky,

and Connor would meet him there.

Connor, the star boy, the one from outer space who brought tales of new adventures and a dazzling smile, as if straight from the sun itself.

Connor, the one who promised that things would be ok as long as the boy never lost sight of the stars.

Inevitably, one day Connor warned the boy of how close he seemed.

"You know this has always just been for fun, I couldn't love you."

The boy broke because for him, Connor wasn't just a lover or a friend, he was his star: the brightest one he had.

So how could he continue visiting the stars

knowing that Connor would always be a
constellation of pain.

The boy promised to cut himself off, like one
with a disease who didn't deserve their
diagnosis.

He realized their relationship was a meteor
destined to strike an unsuspecting planet.

Just because he fell in love with the stars while
nobody else had the courage to look away from
earth.

Connor stopped showing up.

Maybe because the boy stopped looking, or
maybe because Connor didn't want to be found.

However, it seems as if the boy grew tired of
searching the stars for someone he would never
find.

So Connor became nothing more than stardust,
and the boy grew into a man wiser than the
brightest star,

because he had the wisdom of thousands of
galaxies whispering to him

"Remember us the way he forgot you."

a city

this isn't the city you promised me
the one with the lights that sparkle like eyes after
tears have fallen
the one where the girls' hands drive across you
like cars on the highway
the city doesn't shine like the smiles of the
neighbors you wish you lived next to
it isn't the field of flowers i lay in to reminisce
about how it feels to ride on a cloud and listen to
the thunder lullaby

you promised me a city with no curfew, where
adults kiss you and tell you how proud of you
they are regardless of what you've done,
regardless of the mistakes you've made
you're still promised a good time

the boy on fire doesn't melt your heart of ice
buildings don't call my name and whisper

sunset reflections into my ear while i dance
across the skyline

birds sing softer in the nighttime as if they are
scared of being caught
strangled, their cries echo only briefly

alarms blare, asking you to wake up from a
dream that occurs only while you are awake
children don't play on jungle gyms
instead, prisoners are confined to the bars that
represent innocence and freedom
how funny

i've lived in an apartment for years with closets
that i'm scared to open
what if one day, you are waiting for me?
then what would i say
"how dare you sugarcoat your words?"
"how dare you create a hard candy crystal
covered cold castle of lies?"

but truthfully, i would ask myself

"how dare i believe you?"

then, the city limits

i met you there the first time

a barren wasteland filled with your empty

words

pointing in the direction

of all the cities you promised me before locking

the gates and turning your back

encouraging me to stay

before you left

hypotheticals

i'd fall in love with hot coffee and the smell of
books if they were enough to take me back to it
i swear i'm tired of writing about love i've never
been in
but sometimes it's better to pretend you've
experienced something you haven't than accept
that your feelings are 2 dimensional
i could look you in the eyes and swear i love you
and i bet you wouldn't even know if i was lying
i could drive to your house at 4 in the morning
with flowers and my promises that we could
stay together forever but nothing would change
the way my mind races when i picture us
together
the way two comets race together across galaxies
and beyond

i'd fall in love with movies i don't like and
places i've never been if you told me to
if you kissed my cheek and apologized for
everything i assumed you did
i'd probably melt
a little faster than the ice cream we shared on the
dates we've never been on
the ones where you drive a blue convertible with
candy in the cup holders
we hold hands
but only when we're laughing otherwise it
seems forced
i could take you up a flight of stars and fall on
top of you but you still wouldn't be as breathless
as you make me

oh i can feel you deep in my soul
you're a mountain left with the remains of
people who couldn't quite understand you like

i've convinced myself i can
i'd fall in love with knives and dark nights if you
showed me how
my brain gets fuzzy when you're around
because there's too much to process
like the girl your arms are around or the smiles
you share with everyone except me
poison drips from your wounds instead of blood
because that stains and at least poison is still a
weapon

do you read my writing and cower thinking
about how easy it is for me to lock you in
metaphors and descriptions of somebody you
hope you aren't
but how would you know what it's like to watch
you
to listen to you like the playlists i only enjoy
sometimes
you're a mattress i can only sleep on sideways

and i hope one day you'll wake up without me
and call for my name only to be greeted
with the echoes of what could've been

nostalgia (2)

in my neighborhood i always met them at the tree. it was our throne, our base. it was a castle built for tiny monarchs of all shapes and sizes. we met at the tree because it was a safe enough distance from all the parents and everyone could make it alone, undaunted by the climb or the walk as long as their friends were waiting for them.

there was so much waiting back then. waiting to grow up, to move to middle school. we waited for summer and for recess and to meet once again at the tree. little did we know where all that waiting would get us.

one day i visited the tree again. the blossoms didn't seem so vibrant. there was no swing, no friends calling my name. now they were nothing more than faces much older than the images i have stored.

you stop hearing laughter. you start hearing
about college and boys and parties. you start
remembering instead of doing. who knows what
happened in the spaces between youth and
adolescence. who knows when that occurred.

i hate talking about my childhood sadly. i
should be happy about what i experienced at
that tree, the friends i made. sometimes i just
find myself waiting though. waiting at that tree
for a familiar face or my name to be called. i'm
waiting and i'm waiting and suddenly i realized
i'm waiting for something that can't happen.
something so unlike what we used to wait for. so
unlike wanting to grow up, because here i am.
waiting again. only this time, i'm not waiting for
more years or more experience. i'm waiting to
recall how summers used to smell, or when
exactly that tree's limbs died.

it's just me now. sitting on a stump with memories of trees. memories of laughing children flood my brain and my eyes flood too.

how i've missed you, how i've waited to return to the moments that i wanted so badly to be over. stuck in the middle of a city that loved me until i was done waiting and realized how trapped i am.

i miss the tree. i miss my friends. i miss being proud to speak the name of the place i live, i miss being proud to tell everyone how much i loved a tree. i couldn't keep it alive long enough.

leaving your house is like leaving a dream i
never want to wake up from. you never want me
there as much as i do but i still fall asleep every
night hoping i can return.

if i could pack everything about us in an
envelope and ship it to you, or to anyone, i
would. you wouldn't open it for several days but
i can imagine the sticky layers being torn by
your perfect hands and i'm melting over and
over

i wonder how it feels to live in a world where i
am not your you the way you are mine. people
whisper about love in languages i don't
understand but i'm sure you're fluent despite
how badly you don't want to be

you are the only thing that warms my heart in

the winter weather. now i crave snow so that
you can make me feel safer

when i think of you i think of quiet nights and
talking about girls. when i dream of you i dream
of everything else

there is no space and all space between us and i
wonder how many bridges it would take for me
to cross to you and still feel unsatisfied. have
you scanned the river and looked for shallow
parts or are you content to drown?

you may promise you will love me forever but it
won't ever be enough and everyday i will pray
to your god as long as it keeps us together. i'm
so so clingy but i feel that if i ever let go i'd start
falling and never stop.

i left an envelope for you on the table. in it is three hundred dollars, this note, and my whole heart. i figured nobody else would ever own it like you do.

i can imagine your fingers tearing at the sticky layers and im melting; over and over

cruel world

if the whole world is our home, why have i been
confined to one dark corner.
why is my room merely an island in the sea of
your ambition?
you own the sunsets and the trees and the
mountains
i am another child watching the clouds from his
window
and you only remember me when you are lost
again
dancing across the world you gifted yourself
shining among the stars before you notice
little old me
begging for a piece of this world
a piece of your world

lost friend

I took off on my bike again today. Coldest it's been in a while. It's still raining.

I played the songs that I discovered after you. I'm so jealous of the way they don't know your name. Or your smile.

I wasn't even sure if I wanted to put on my helmet. Nothing protected me from this, the way it feels when your tears and your rain mix to create a cocktail even more poisonous than the ones people drink to forget. The only haze I find myself in is filled with memories I'm tired of remembering.

I saw the sign for the place I first remember going with you. So young then, so ignorant. My mother pointed it out first. Not as the place we went to, but as the place she used to love. What a coincidence.

I've been alone in these woods for too long now.
I knew they would only be colder, but my skin
might be the warmest part of me now. My mind
is almost numb

Back near the train tracks that remind me too
much of years passed. Nostalgia built into wood
planks and a loud wake up call whistle. I used to
come here and dream of you.

How silly I must be to everyone else. How silly I
am to myself. When people ask why I miss you
so much, I can't ever tell them because I'm to
busy rolling the tears out of my eyes.

I'm so exhausted with trying to move on. Maybe
I've reached the end, and we only really get one.
Maybe you're the one who will be my writer's
muse forever. Are you happy you're

immortalized on paper and in my heart?

I don't hesitate to stand up and scream. No sound except for the roar of my blood and the rain again. Reminds me of the water at your house, the place I haven't seen in years except in my mind. How are your blood-red sheets?

I'm picking my bicycle up again. Nothing has changed except the temperature of the rain. It's coming down harder now. Urging me to get up and leave before I remember more about you.

I guess that's it then. Pedaling again. There's no conclusion this time either. There never is. There may never be.

pick yourself up

not for anyone else

maybe not even for yourself

only because if you don't

who will?

- **what then**

brother nature

i am nature
my arms are tree limbs, full and lively and fresh
and strong
my legs are mountains, tall and thick and
rugged
my skeleton is a forest, hundreds of unbreakable
beams in a collection of beauty

river water flows through my veins and you can
hear the call of the wild if you listen to my
heartbeat
my hair is a field of tall grass, the kind children
dance through under the moonlight
a bee nest resides in my skull, thousands of
thoughts swarming around like an
uncontrollable collective

i have the voice of a canary and the intelligence
of a fox and the beauty of millions of flowers

mother nature birthed me from her womb and
since then my roots have grown straight to her
core

your words are machines that will never
compare to the valleys in my skin and the oceans
in my eyes
you cannot manufacture the purity that comes
from the ethereal

never

there was never a place for them
there was a place for him
and a place for her
but when they combined,
it was as if two start had met
powerful,
yet destructive

oh red

in apples, you are sweet and tempting
plucked from trees; perfectly round and
tempting
shoved in lunch boxes and grandmother's pie
you are innocence

Spain:
you are anger and passion
a bull's kick, visualized
a flag waving in the breeze
you are anger

sunsets bring rays painted by god's brush
vibrant and bold
a circle of mystery and wonder
a promise to return; left on the horizon
you are beauty

faces hold you captive
flushed with passion
hot tears of laughter
you are human

burning brighter than all lights
yet still dark as night
loud and scarring
sweaty and uncomfortable
you are fire

oh red
how dare you place yourself
everywhere you don't deserve to be
in my hands and in my mouth and in my mind
and even in my heart
and yet
somehow
you always leave me wanting more

promises

foggy air and sweaty bodies
murky thoughts and wandering emotions
a boy and a girl
nothing between them except meaningless
desire

i begged you not to
i drowned you in pleads and she promised
he promised
they promised

as her lips met his i wonder if she tasted me like
blood or, perhaps
 your sour regret was more prominent

i wonder if his hair feels softer when her mind is
swirling with chemicals

i wonder if her body seems more fragile to him,
the way flower stems seem to break when you
find yourself in a field you see no beauty in

of course she knew
every ounce of me was there, with her,
despite the distance between us
and he couldn't help but think about
the last time he saw my face before he turned his
back

two people whose desires outweighed their
morals
and who am i to control what goes on behind
closed doors
however, every time i see their faces touch in my
mind i can hear my heart skip a beat

and why?

why has my life momentarily become so
enraging
why have two of those closest to me ruined what
i've always been so attached to
it is as if their bond is a knife;
cutting through invincible ties
how dare this weaken me so much
how dare i be stripped down to nothing without
my consent
how dare she
how dare he
how dare they

sleepy

i imagine your face only looks more beautiful in the morning light and because of that i am so terrified of your droopy eyes and your sleepy smile; knowing that waking up next to you will only bring me pain, recognizing the padlock around your heart and your body and that the password is the only thing about you that i am unable to memorize

t r a p s

i've always been placed in boxes
quick evaluations that lead to seemingly perfect
c o n c l u s i o n s
good, b a d, nice, mean
pretty, ugly, dangerous, safe
0 1 0 1 0 0 1 1

thousands of words,
e v e r y o n e is a series of numbers, n o t h i n g
else
an unbreakable binary

but still there remains everything you cannot
chart and graph and tie up with a bow
no numbers exist that accurately show the way
your eyes sparkle in the middle of a laugh

no language can express smiles other than the
crinkles at the corners of your face and even
music notes seem unnecessary when the
speakers blast an anthem

and so how can raw emotion and the true
human experience be placed in a box with no
room to breathe
 it is impossible to classify all the diversity of this
beautiful earth

truthfully, your classification can come from
nobody except your own mind and heart
no 1's and no 0's will ever represent you better
than the colors and sights and sounds that make
up your life

never needed cocaine

i had you instead

your lips

were

the greatest high i could've asked for

\-   **cravings**

savor it

life is an ice cream cone

often disappointing
often sticky
often sweet
and of course, always melting

you start with so much left, telling yourself how
much time remains between you and the end
so you enjoy it liberally, not savoring the taste
like your parents warn you to
because, they say, "you aren't getting another."
you roll your eyes. why would you need another
with so much left?

as you continue, things seem to thin. not only do the remains dwindle, but the taste seems bland and repetitive and maybe you're questioning where it all went. your parents once again advise you about how fast you are consuming what is not everlasting. they comment on how seemingly little time has elapsed since the beginning. you roll your eyes.

people pass by you and you may wave but you are too focused on the satisfaction that comes with every bite. it is melting more and more, drip by drip falling away and you wish you could savor each and every one. you fail though, because for you, you've only just begun. how could so much be gone so quickly?

your parents left you now. wherever they are,
they no longer offer any advice. you're left with
a murky sticky mess to deal with by yourself.
little opportunity and excitement remains. you
look around and are saddened by how fast it all
seemed to end, how fast you finished what you
told yourself would last forever.

with a deep breathe you discard your ice cream.
you toss it into a trash can, close your eyes, and
sigh

familiarity

i built my house in a place it would not forever
rest peacefully
my hands worked thousands of years to contruct
a temple in a valley filled with narrowed eyes
from small minded strangers and it has been
forever yet my mind does not forget the smell of
the trees or the sounds of mankind's
development that floated through the windows

i built a house within someone else's,
surrounded by family that was not my own
while convincing myself i belonged
i fell asleep to the sounds of someone else's
favorite songs and promised that i liked it
despite how out of place i was

i built a house on the top of a building in a city
that i never wanted to live in
i looked hundreds of strangers in the eyes
everyday and never even asked how they were
i made breakfast among the clouds and yet still i
was unsatisfied

i built a house in someone's heart
bricks were laid in a place they were never
meant to rest
i knew, this time, that i would always be happy
here but of course, that was far too much to ask
for
as everything pulsed around me, walls fell apart
faster than i ever could've anticipated

my home resides everywhere it should not
i have danced across living rooms with
unfamiliar furniture and rested between walls
that i didn't even bother to decorate.

i wonder if i will ever fit into a space as perfectly
as everyone else does
i wonder where i belong, and who i belong with
i believe that i could build thousands of houses
and still would never feel comfortable

perhaps, then, it is not the building that defines
home
instead it is the feelings that come from being
surrounded by those you trust and the aches of
your face from smiling too much or gasping for
air after laughing for hours

i would build a house in every city in the world
still i wish to be happy rather than comfortable
a house is nothing but a space,
a home is everything but

lipreading

my mind was always something you didn't
want to understand

some days i was poetry that you were not
interested in reading
some days i was a stop sign, but you were
always speeding
some days i am a dancer. and still you are
leading

thousands of warnings that we were never
heeding
never seemed to notice that neither of us were
succeeding

a time existed when i longed for you to look into
my heart, nod your head, and smile
i used to wait so patiently
but now i'm simply pleading

when my soul has passed and nothing remains
of me except what the ground has claimed
bring my belongings to the streets of new york
city where hopefully they will feel a sense of
familiarity. they will know that they have found
their way back home and brought every bit of
me with them

you loved us

but i loved you

only you

½ of the equation was missing

- **that's why**

float

have you ever pictured yourself as driftwood?
i know the metaphor sounds silly of course
but imagine for a moment

you are rough and bruised and battered,
unforgiving as you begin a journey across the
sea of life
with each rock and pull of the tides you are
shaped
how smooth you are slowly becoming
the moon rises every night to watch your
drifting slumber
and again and again you are peeled back,
smoothed by life's harsh lessons and her salty
advice

finally you have arrived
a beach pulls you in after year and years of
transformation

life has done you so well
you stand anew, shining in the sun as you are
cleansed for the last time
prepared and ready
ready to take on the earth

paper goddess

isn't she beautiful?

the woman, she's here with us

her skin is pale and her hair is stiff but her

tattoos are stunning

she grasps your hand and she does not need to

utter a thing

you are already comfortable in her grip

her dress is silk and her arms stretch miles and

miles

perhaps if you ask kindly, she will show you

what i've told her about you

i never forbid her from it

coax her into staying with you and maybe she

will whisper lullabies from any poet's own

mouth

she is dreamy isn't she

can't you see yourself in her dark eyes

so subtly being for more of her

you told yourself you weren't interested in the
art of poetry but you can't avert your gaze when
it's right in front of you,
can you?
don't you want to know what happens next?
don't you want to know how it ends?
lay with her a while
you won't ever look back

suddenly there was no space between us

and despite everything i know about you

i am falling

so, so fast

- inevitably

my mouth waters at the sight of cinnamon

i crave the way

you expect sugar

and receive fire instead

i take comfort knowing i will be burned

- **pleasure?**

centerpiece

i'm sitting at a dinner party that i didn't want to
be invited to
everything is porcelain
everyone tells me how handsome i look
they ask if i have a girlfriend
i smile and laugh and shake my head
i think of the boys i've been in love with
everything is porcelain
every utensil is perfectly in line
funny how despite the perfection of it all
it still remains destructible
everything is porcelain
my plate is shiny and smooth
begging for someone to put food on it
but it didn't really get a say in what kind
white teeth white napkins white walls
white people
everything is porcelain
they smile and ask about school

i smile and hate every bit of it
but how would they know
i've never had the chance to tell them over the
sounds of future colleges and sports teams i
don't like
someone leans in and offers me a hug
i don't know them
everything is porcelain
my tie is a noose that someone else tied for me
my pants are scratchy and uncomfortable
just like everything else
there's a vase of flowers in the center of the long
wooden table; it is porcelain
and i forget whether i have been invited
or if i am being forced to stay
like flowers
in a porcelain vase

Neon Highs

A short story to conclude *everything*

I roll my car window up as I pull into the alley next to Neon Club. Wind abruptly ceases to whip through my hair and it saddens me a little. If I was anyone else, the bouncers would flip their shit about my parking, but nobody else has been a regular at this club since they could walk. Eve is inside waiting for me like she always is. My leather jacket protects me from the chilly New York weather as I make my way to the front of the building. I nod to the same beefy guy I've known for years, still have no idea what to call him. The bar is semi-crowded, but most people are on the dance floor. I scan the crowd and only recognize a few people. Sigh. I head to our corner at the back with the white couches.

"Alex!" a voice cries. I flick my eyes away from the dancing blurs and find Eve already rolling her eyes at my outfit. She thinks the jacket makes me look like an asshole. I'd say my fashion sense matches my personality. Not to mention this was my dad's. Eve doesn't know that though. She's not the kind of person I'm willing to talk to about that kind of stuff. I lean down and give her a kiss.

"How's everything tonight?" She knows I'm referring to the club's atmosphere. She's a little spacy. She's probably had a few drinks while she was waiting for me.

"It's been ok. They aren't here yet,

though, and I was feeling kinda awkward all alone." "They" are Bryce and Spark, the other half of our little group. I guess they're a couple, but a better description of them would be two halves of the same soul. They're the definition of "perfect for each other." It doesn't surprise me that they aren't here yet considering that Spark makes Bryce take the bus to "save the environment" and they can't ever accomplish it without arguing for thirty minutes first.

"We can go ahead and order some drinks," I tell Eve, and she smiles. It's her favorite part of coming to Neon. Even I'll admit, the drinks are pretty cool. They glow. Like, the liquid literally shines through the cups. Some kind of edible neon powder they mix in. Whatever it is, they do a lot more than just make the drink glow, and they're totally worth the expensive admission into the club. Which, of course, doesn't apply to Eve, Bryce, Spark, or me.

"Go sit down, I'll get our usual," I say to Eve.

"Ok. I want orange this time though." As if I hadn't already figured out her pattern. Orange one week, yellow the next. And still every time she acts like I wouldn't have known that without her telling me. Like I said, spacey.

She's not beautiful. Not like Anna was. Eve is pretty and sweet, but I know there's no future between us. I guess me saying that really is something an asshole would say, but nobody will ever compare to Anna. Eve is a temporary pleasure that isn't enough to fill the hole that Anna left when she left. For now though, Eve is ok.

Bryce and Spark catch me at the bar and I'm not surprised to see they're the best dressed in the whole club by far. There aren't many gay stereotypes they fit besides being able to dress, but I would never tell them that because I don't want to give Spark the satisfaction. He's wearing black pants that seem to shimmer every time he moves. At first glance, his sleeveless shirt is also black, but when any of the neon lights of the club catch it, the fabric reflects them back even brighter. I'm not even sure how that's physically possible.

"Wow, I wonder who's this dark, mysterious guy at the bar?" Bryce jokingly raises his voice to say to Spark. I roll my eyes. Bryce is such a smartass. Before he met Spark, it was just he and I. He won't admit it, but he had the biggest crush on me back then. We lived in the same house and sometimes when I brought girls over he would break down and just not talk to me for the whole day. It never bothered me, but I'm really glad he's with Spark now.

"Nice to see you both too," I respond as

I grab Eve's and my drinks, "She's waiting for y'all." They both make their way towards their couch, and I follow behind. Bryce and Spark both like to dance a little before having any drinks. I guess they appreciate both sober and drunk fun. The four of us make small talk about our weeks as Eve and I finish our first drinks. Bryce ditches his denim jacket at the corner as the four of us make our way down to the dance floor. The DJ is absolutely killing it tonight, and I wish I could enjoy it without thinking of the first time I brought Anna here. She was wearing yellow that night, and she glowed brighter than any artificial light in here.

Bryce and Spark fly around the floor, and you'd be an idiot not to move out of the way of their twists and turns. No matter the genre of the song, leave it to them to have some synchronized choreography for it. They never fail to impress everyone in the club, and they're part of the reason Neon Club invested in higher quality floors about a year ago.

Eve grabs me and I can tell she wants me to hold her as this next slow song begins. I obediently allow her to bury herself in my arms and we sway back and forth. It all seems so superficial to me. Back when I used to work here, there weren't so many lovesick couples on the dance floor. People came to Neon for good times, and just like the slogan says, to "Leave it in the dark." Now, there are so many drunk underage teenagers around that you'd think this was the only bar in town. We're in New York City, for god's sake. I swear if there's a place in this town worth anything at all, teenagers will ruin it.

"I need some air," I announce to the group. All three of them look shocked, I guess I'm not really one to "need air." Especially not at Neon. What they don't know is that I just wanted a second to see the skyline. You'd think after 5 years in New York that I'd be over all the twinkling lights from hundreds of buildings, but you'd be wrong. I'm especially fond of the way it looks from Neon Club, which provides one of the best views in town. As I shove past a homeless guy who's probably about to get asked to leave, I turn my attention to the sky.

I can feel the drinks fogging my mind now. My brain is processing everything slowly and I almost forget what I was doing out here. I take a seat on the curb and glance around the street, admiring the way the buildings sparkle even just next to me.

I remember Anna talking about the city. It's probably one of the reasons I like it so much. It was one of our last real conversations.

"Why do people complain about a lack of stars here if they have this instead?" She asked me, genuinely confused.

"I don't know," I responded. I couldn't help but smile a little as she said that. I hate smiling. It's like an invitation for people to assume things about you.

We looked out from my balcony for one of the last times as she placed her hand on mine on the railing. Her long dark hair fluttered in the winds as a siren went off somewhere a few streets over. I kissed her, also for one of the last times. She smelled like lavender.

"Seriously though, I bet half the people in New York don't even realize what they're missing. They just go about their nights either sleeping or watching TV but if they just looked out their window every now and then, maybe things would be different." She decided as she pulled away.

"Maybe people are scared. A lot of people probably don't want to be left alone with just their thoughts and thousands and thousands of lights."

I snapped back into reality as I realized that is exactly what I am. Alone among the lights. I should definitely get back inside. They're already suspicious enough. I take one last look out at the city before slipping in the door through some idiot's cigarette smoke.

As I make my way across the floor back to our little group, I can't help but think that Anna was upset about people's inability to see what's right in front of them because she, too, knew she was missing something.

Hopefully she's found it by now.

Made in the USA
Lexington, KY
27 August 2018